THE GREAT BOOK OF
MOBILE TALK

THE GREAT BOOK OF
MOBILE TALK

'You like mashed potato, don't you?'

Overheard by ANDREW BARROW
Observed by POSY SIMMONDS

■ SQUARE PEG

Published by Square Peg 2013

2 4 6 8 10 9 7 5 3 1

Copyright © Andrew Barrow 2013

Illustration copyright © Posy Simmonds 2013

First published in Great Britain in 2013 by
Square Peg
Random House, 20 Vauxhall Bridge Road,
London SW1V 2SA

www.vintage-books.co.uk

Addresses for companies within The Random House Group Limited can
be found at:
www.randomhouse.co.uk/offices.htm

The Random House Group Limited Reg. No. 954009

A CIP catalogue record for this book is available from the British Library

ISBN 9780224095624

The Random House Group Limited supports The Forest Stewardship
Council® (FSC®), the leading international forest-certification organisation.
Our books carrying the FSC label are printed on FSC®-certified paper.
FSC is the only forest-certification scheme supported by the leading
environmental organisations, including Greenpeace. Our paper
procurement policy can be found at
www.randomhouse.co.uk/environment

Typeset in Bembo by Palimpsest Book Production Ltd, Falkirk, Stirlingshire
Printed and bound in Great Britain by Clays Ltd, St Ives plc

THE GREAT BOOK OF
MOBILE TALK

Hello? All right? Can you hear me?

*I think that's one thing we **can** agree about*

Good morning! I wonder if you can help me?

You like mashed potato, don't you?

Which way are you spelling that?

I can't read my own writing. I've written down half past three on Friday. Can that be right?

Sorry, we went into a tunnel

In other words, I'm fucked basically

Ten quid an hour? No way!

*Hello? Hello? Oh, you **are** there! Excellent!*

It's my third day without alcohol

You don't know what Sheila's doing on Tuesday, do you?

Name of your road again?

[1]

Haven't a clue!

I'm going to compete with Jade and become the super-tidy mother of the year

When would she be available after that?

It's my mission in life

Hi, it's me! Mary!

I'm afraid he loves the sound of his own voice

I've got here already! I'm outside now!

That's something she won't forget in a hurry

She won't sell that flat in a hurry

And I'm working all day on Sunday. So I'm not going to get a lie-in till next Saturday

I'm going to see You Know Who tonight!

[2]

I don't find Pete attractive at all. My mother is convinced we're going to get married

Are you still annoyed with me?

Where are you now?

And this is all with the old woman, Jane, with the short hair?

I can hardly hear you!

I went absolutely berserk. By that stage we were losing five–one

*Now I'm worried because I'm going to Florida. And **he's** going to be in Florida too!*

Is that Gordon?

Pardon?

If that's Gordon, can we speak a bit later?

I like the blighter and I intend to make it obvious

[4]

They're basically going to be filming
between eleven and two

Paris was murder!

Darling Mary, it's Sal. I couldn't get
you on your mobile but I **have** got you
a preserving pan. Just to let you know

*Besides which, I've got a lot of work
to do*

Don't even think about it!

*I know you've far, far better things
to do but I would love to have a
word with you sometime*

You all right, mate?

I never let it upset me, honestly

Perhaps I can drop it off on you later?
Would there be anyone at
one o'clock? Please let me
know

*Ring me up, Tom,
if and when
you've got a moment*

[5]

Maybe tonight we could go to a movie?

When I was last in Bahrain, I stayed in a fucking big house

Okay, that would be good

I'll speak to you in a sec!

I can be with you in five minutes if you want!

Who's this latest man? You've teased me now

I'm just ringing up to find out if I can pop round this evening and sort it out?

I'm just around the corner!

Have you got pen and paper?

There's no point asking him. He's an idiot

SORRY, I'VE JUST ELBOWED SOMEBODY! WHOOPSY!

Why do you hate me?

I can't believe you just said that!

I said I'm just around the corner!

 His profile has got to
have gone up in the last
few months, hasn't it?

*It's going to solve my
entire financial
predicament*

Shall we make a date for Jane and Pete
to come over for supper? We could have
them with Nick and Anna, because we
owe them one too, don't we?

Meaning what exactly?

I don't trust you guys

What are you trying to say?

I was just ringing to say hello. Don't
bother to ring back. I just wanted to
say hello. Nothing important

Yes, I had a quick chat with Sharon

He owes me, like, ten grand

[8]

I can't hear a word you're saying

Plus, it looks horrible

Who the hell does she think she is?

It's Gemma and it's now – oh gosh, what time is it? – twenty to ten. I was in the shower when you rang. I'm now on the way to the bank

Friday. Twenty past two. Are you all right? I'll try your mobile

How's your hip doing? Do you ignore it now?

Just ringing to say that Pete and I will do anything to help. Anything, anything, anything!

Some of us have to work tomorrow

She didn't look very well last time I saw her. In fact, she looked absolutely shattered

We just need to keep her from falling over and hurting herself

[9]

Or am I mad?

You didn't miss much last night!

I'm almost at your flat now!

D'you want me to bring my computer?

I've just left a parcel on your doorstep!

I'm just going to have a little tidy-uppy

I'm not sure if you got my text

After that I'll be at home all day with no plans

I think you ought to take the antibiotics just in case

I've got more than one friend. Thank you very much

I'll buy the veggies!

Well, they obviously don't need the money, do they? I mean, Mary's got her own money too, hasn't she?

So you make sympathetic noises?

Oh, come off it, Malcolm!

Have the kids been good? Oh, bless him! I'll let you go. Bye!

I'm kind of resigning from the whole thing

I left my phone in the car. I meant to ring you earlier

People were paying silly money, weren't they?

The awful thing is I don't agree with you. I love the Church of England

You're not going to grow a beard in only one day!

Anyway, we'll see

I've got to ring bloody Gordon now!

The car door was so badly smashed they had to climb out of the window

They seem to be living entirely for pleasure

No, but that's adorable! I'm so happy for you guys!

One thing I want to ask you. One thing I want to tell you

And are we then going out to eat?

He's got a younger brother, hasn't he?

I know who you're talking about but I don't know him personally

Some of the things I know would astound you

He's a phoney fucking idiot!

The party's off, by the way

You're all hung up with these idiot people!

Ah, yes. You can do me a favour. Ring Jackie and say it's all right about last night. I spent the night at your place

He was dropping names all over the place

I'm getting deeper and deeper into a mess

He eventually got the message I wasn't interested

She broke a heavy ashtray on my spine

I'm just going to buy an umbrella

You've got to get a hold on yourself, Jackie, and stop worrying about my mother. She's ten thousand miles away!

I couldn't give a fuck!

Oh, for fuck's sake, it was a mistake

Shut up and go away!

There are lots of blokes with banners coming up the street!

FUCK OFF!

It's common sense. I buy the best packet I can and flavour it with cream and butter

I can't stand people who lie in bed all day

I'm getting a lock fitted to the fridge!

I'm not altogether a fool

I'm not going to divulge any more to you

How is the wicked Uncle James?

How do you know Nicky Haslam?

I left my new umbrella in the Turk's Head yesterday and I'm terribly upset about it

D'you like red cabbage? Ask Eva if she likes red cabbage

Oh, Christ, I left the damned gallery lights on!

JUST TALKING OUT LOUD. PAY NO ATTENTION

[16]

I told her to wait for me where I was going to be but she didn't listen

Sorry to bother you but do you like red cabbage?

Let the dust settle a little bit

See you later, babe!

*It's William. We're running terribly late but we'll be there in ten minutes. Sorry about that. Thank you **so** much*

Bring a sketch pad!

And where are we going to meet? Back at the tube station?

OH, MY GOD!

What d'you make of the new look? Everyone else loves it

I haven't felt like this for ages!

I can't remember the exact measurements

I don't know at all. We don't talk about things like that

> *How about a bite of lunch?*

There were chocolate eggs everywhere!

> *I'll see you tomorrow if I may*

I'm not unduly worried at the moment. D'you know what I mean?

> *Hello, Andy. Did you just call me? I'm on my way to the Dog and Duck now. Sorry? Hello?*

Always make sure Gordon knows everything

> ***Where are you? Tesco's? Oh my God!***

Are you drunk?

> *I'll double-check. I'll give her a call now*

I'll never be able to trust you again!

There has to be a better way to get to this place!

You're right. I was in hospital. Recovering

*How are **you**, anyway?*

Sorry I interrupted. You were about to say something really interesting

I just can't go on with it. I just can't. I know. I know. I know

D'you know what I mean, Mark?

Just a minute, Tim

Okay, Hugo, I'll see you tomorrow

We went from Hanoi to Colum Bay in one day. Not bad?

If he can't bring out the best in a woman he's not much of a man

Which is like an island off the coast of California. No, a little beach hut. No, actually, we took the ferry. It was quite tricky actually

[20]

My sister's boyfriend is under the impression she's away

> *Nobody really knows what they're talking about*

If I married you, I would destroy your life

> *On the way back we took a propeller plane! And I was sat next to the propeller!*

I like the name Tom. It's simple but nice

> *I've had loads and loads of parking tickets!*

I've now got to wait around for the results

> **You're joking!**

Darling, sweethearts. Don't know where you are. It would be great to catch you before I zoom down to Dorking. I'll try again later

I gave up all that years ago!

I'm probably disturbing you

> *It's just Mary. I was just*
> *wondering what tube stop it is.*
> *Don't worry. I'll find out myself*

He now avoids me on every occasion

> *Just to say I've now got these people*
> *coming to supper tomorrow night*

It's ten past five. I'll call you in twenty minutes

> *I just hope everything went well*
> *yesterday. No need to call back*

What about some of those nice finger-shaped dry biscuits?

> *I'll try you again in a few minutes*

Everybody knows Nicky Haslam

> *I'm sorry, I can hardly hear you*

Hello, it's Mary again. I think my last message may have been cut off

How do you spell that?

I couldn't tell you,
dear

*I just wondered if you'd all like
croissants tomorrow morning. I'll get
some anyway*

Early evening would be good. Say, after
five o'clock

Lots and lots of love anyway!

That's what's so stupid

*One extremely minor point of detail
which is that my office is actually
in Victoria rather than Parsons
Green*

I think it's valiant of you to do this

*Oh yes, and the number you gave
my mother doesn't work*

Go on. Say it!

It'll be a laugh, if nothing else

I was ringing with the idea in mind of
– oh, damn, I've gone and left my
diary somewhere! Oh, gosh, I'm so
sorry! I'll have to ring you back!

> *Perhaps you could ring me back
> sometime?*

I don't necessarily expect you to ring
me back immediately

> *Do get a copy of the* Daily Mail
> *today. It's quite interesting. Page
> twenty-three*

THE POT OF HONEY HAS ARRIVED!

> *I've got a bad cold. Do give me a
> ring. Lots of love. Goodbye*

Sweetie-pie, do give me a ring when
you can. It's just that I need you to
bring the tablets which are on the
surface, near the drinks
tray

> *Where's your
> boyfriend, then?*

He's a can of worms! Watch him! He's gone bankrupt more times than I can remember

OK, mate, no problem. Cheers, mate!

If you change your mind, let me know

Darling, I'm sorry but Katie didn't sleep very well last night and is now a bit under the weather

Obviously, *all* of you are welcome

So can we reschedule tea?

He's been away ten days and hasn't rung me once!

It's six thirty. I've been trying to get you on and off all day

Just saying hello. Talk to you soon

I just don't know where you are or whether you're out?

I slept last night in Grandpa's bed!

Probably best not to repeat that

Sounds good!

She's got the whole thing buggered up actually, but who am I to say it?

What a shocking summer! We'll have a baking hot winter, that's what'll happen

That's what I mean. It's all innuendoes

I said to Mary I wish I'd put a cardigan on

Marvellous, innit? I said could I speak to Mr Uke? They said, no you can't. He died last night!

Hello, cutie-pie!

Part two. From Gordon. Could you give me a ring sometime? Nothing urgent

Then they loaded me up with a whole lot of chicken breasts. Which I hadn't asked for

Tell me. What's the problem?

You're freaking me out!

If you've got a car, you could park it near Waitrose and we could grab a bit of food

Did you hear what Corinne said about me on Twitter?

Oh, you haven't got a car?

When I mentioned the food situation, you didn't sound too happy about it

There's still no sign of life from next door

I'm sure they would if you asked them

I wouldn't mind having salmon

I don't quite understand it

I don't know what it is but there's something about you I can't help liking

[29]

Sorry about last night!

> *And you're running out of loo
> paper, my darling!*

Seems feasible to me

> *There's a new bit of kit that's just
> been delivered that could solve all
> our problems*

We saw this Italian guy being pulled
into the water by crocodiles!

> *I was her first customer when she
> opened*

Don't be so horrible!

> *I asked you to do me a favour and
> you immediately tried to palm it off
> onto Sheila*

D'you like cash?

> *If that makes sense*

If you add on veg suppliers, meat
suppliers, that's another eight grand

*In that case I will be employing
a large bloke to go and kill
him!*

I was just hoping to speak to my big
sister

*And that was it. End of
conversation*

SORRY ABOUT THAT. I WAS JUST
BALANCING ON THE RAILING
WITH MY OTHER HAND!

*You'd better check his food in case
he tries to poison us all!*

So I'll see you just after two o'clock?

*She gets furious whenever you
mention it*

That's got to be an indication of
something

*The reason I wanted to delay our
conversation until now is that I
needed to talk to Lorna Low first*

Don't try any funny business!

[32]

*Do you have children? I thought I
could hear a child laughing in the
background*

You mean this week?

So far, I'm as pleased as punch

I do, yes. Four. Zero. Eight. Five

*This is exactly what I said to
Lorna*

Not that I've been to Mauritius but I
imagine it's quite nice

What I was thinking was –

OH, MY GOD, I FORGOT TO FEED
THE GUINEA PIGS!

You're leading the life of a rock star!

You're stressing me out!

I'll check it out and get back to you

Hello, Lee. You all right, mate?

*Are you going to do the toilet this
afternoon?*

[33]

I can't stand flies. I'd sooner have a spider than a fly. They get up to all sorts of things, flies

If the murder squad get involved at the
last moment –

>   *I'll definitely see you at Mike
>   Davis's*

At the moment they're up the road at
number three four five

>   *Hi, mate! I've got you now!
>   Listen, Michael, there's a lot of
>   work to do. Hello? Michael?*

She's turned into a snake!

>   *He was never any good at it*

He done well, then, didn't he?

>   *D'you have any croissants at all?
>   Shall I buy some croissants?*

I said to him the other day he should
buy some new jeans

>   *I can't believe it!*

We were having a giggle about it
down at the pub

*AND LOO
PAPER!*

The hot water
cylinder's now
bust!

*I am happy to go ahead with things
once we've got all the costings*

I'm not your servant!

*He's bedridden now. You have to
walk through his bedroom to get to
the lounge*

Cool!

Twenty-five years I've known Lorna

Listen, mate, if you died tomorrow –

*All the double-glazed units should
be there by now. Oh, no, they don't
arrive till tomorrow!*

It's not the cleverest thing to do, in all
fairness

SHIT!

[36]

I hear the party was a great success

> *We should have won the*
> *Champions League!*

He should just chill out

> *She's got ownership of the bloody*
> *house. He's done his absolute nuts.*
> *Spent all that money doing it up!*

You know I like mashed potato.
But I don't want to have mashed
potato every single bloody night!

> *How funny! Oh, really? Wow!*

Good memory, Alice!

> *Marble floors! Everything!*

I spent a bit too much of the weekend
staring at the computer screen

> *Somebody still*
> *needs to sort out*
> *the costings!*

No, that would make
sense, actually

[37]

Sasha looked fantastic. She doesn't seem to have changed at all

Was this a long time ago or recently?

Thank you for your card this morning. It made me smile

I'll ring again about this and that. Lovely to speak to you! Take care!

Poor Ma! I'm not surprised. Oh, Ma!

Dad, it's Nick here. Give me a call back

Can you spare a second?

Oh, gosh, I haven't heard of her for a long time

Hello, mate. Are you all right? I'm knackered!

You're joking!

You need to have a verbal agreement, don't you?

Anyway, I'm going to see you in an hour's time

[39]

HOLD ON! HOLD ON! HOLD ON!

She's only about fifty but she's already had her face lifted four times!

It's really weird the way he does that

Guess who I've just seen – Boris Johnson!

Excuse me, but you're talking to me like I'm an idiot. I explained all this on the fifteenth

I said I've just seen Boris Johnson! On the fucking underground!

You can't help seeing the funny side to it

HOW MANY TIMES HAVE I GOT TO GO ON REPEATING THE SAME THING FOR IT TO REGISTER WITH YOU?

No one even knows his name. Dick or Mick or something

[40]

I seem to have been having such rotten luck recently

This was — oh, Christ — twenty-four years ago

In the meantime, what if she finds out about me?

It's a grim old world, John

I always thought you were a bit of a dark horse

I can't stand flies. I'd sooner have a spider than a fly. They get up to all sorts of things, flies

I crawled back to town about midnight

That guy gives me the shits

He was getting a bit shirty at one moment

He's taken a bit of a shine to her

Anyway, a spider is not an insect. It's a mini-beast

It's a thought, isn't it?

That peanut thing we had last night was
very good. Let's have it again tonight

> *That was silly*

I woke up this morning and could
hardly get out of bed!

> *What can we do about it?*

I mean some of those bugs can hang
about for months, can't they?

> *It's the most disgusting thing I've
> ever eaten! Gross!*

If a moth landed on it, it would fall to
pieces. It can't last long. No way

> *They don't normally bite but they
> irritate*

Some people have got a nerve!

> *I don't normally do this kind of
> thing*

It's not our problem

*To be honest, Cath,
I'm in a car and I've
got to get to work*

Oceans of love,
sweetie. I adore you!

I consider that an insult

I quite like housework actually

Really?

Obviously there are some bits which
drive you to distraction

Just when you least expect it!

I like washing and ironing best because
you have a nice end product

I thought, Christ, do I look that old?

Nobody's seen him. He's disappeared
off the face of the earth

She's a little devil, she really is

John always comes out with these little
gems

I'm just going quietly bonkers

I'll take your word for it!

Actually, they're absolutely essential to the running of the household

You're not sounding very convincing, actually

So are you very far from Aldeburgh and Saxmundham?

Have you seen our friend recently?

Why am I telling you this?

SORRY, I'M NOW ON A TRAIN!

That's where the trouble begins!

My name's Lauretta. Just tell her that I'm looking forward to getting her letter

You know the girl I mean?

You can get your filthy hands off her
for a start!

D'you follow?

I've forgotten the name of your road
again!

*It was belting down with rain so I
said, no, I wouldn't bother*

I've known Paul for years now. I know
the way he thinks

I thought we'd eat in tonight

I'm reading your little mind

I imagine his car's broken down again

Let's just eat what's in the fridge!

How's everything at the flat?

It annoyed me intensely

*When you've got someone weighing
eighteen stone sitting on your head
it's no joke*

What happened?

Now, did you say you've got a garden?

I don't think I quite know what you mean

She turned it into two flats

Does anyone know where he's hanging out?

What about Wednesday?

She took ill in the street!

The industrial cleaners are now coming at one thirty but once they've said hello we could go out for a sort of late lunch

Was she taking medicine for it?

He owned the whole of Colorado. All the gold mines, all the diamond mines

He thought the world of you

I think she's a bit shell-shocked by it all. She keeps forgetting what she's saying mid-sentence

You must be bored!

You can't say fairer than that

She's been wonderful to those kids. Never forgets their birthdays

In theory, I have chemotherapy on Wednesday

I've never seen her laugh. I've never seen her enjoy herself

I had no idea he'd turn out so peculiar

Brian Ellis managed to wangle quite good accommodation last time

I get the impression I'm the only person who's learnt from history

Did I tell you that terrible Japanese girl rang up?

You'll laugh! The only person who's rung up and accepted so far is John Adams!

I thank you, my friend

I must dash back to work!

I've been pinched for parking

> *Excellent news, sweetie. Masses of love!*

Give me a ring and I'll give you the details

> *Naughty! Naughty! Naughty!*

Stop being such a baby!

> I'M DESPERATE! WHY ARE YOU NEVER THERE?

She's never done a thing like this before

> *Who's the Shadow Education man?*

I'm afraid I went and had a bit of a holiday

[52]

*I went into the Putney branch and
they didn't have any vacancies*

If you really want to know I went to
sleep again

Are you sure you're okay?

We all like sex, do me a favour

All I say is be bloody careful!

A little bit of John goes a long way

*I had a row with this woman in the
park. She said did I believe in Jesus
Christ. I said, Well, no, I don't*

Hello, babe! I've been trying to get
you for ten days!

*She said why not. I said, Well,
look at the facts!*

D'you remember Jean and
Bernard What's-their-
name?

*D'you understand
what I'm trying to say to you?*

[53]

COME ON, GORDON, FORGET IT! FOR GOD'S SAKE!

> *Apparently she fell out of a taxi when she was pissed!*

Stay at home as long as you like. I'm not complaining!

> *She's a chatterbox but she **is** sweet*

As I said, I'm going to play everything by ear

> *I saw you as a left-winger. Lots of clever sidesteps*

I cannot stay in that house any longer because the atmosphere is so ghastly!

> *It's a good networking opportunity*

Chelmsford's a place I've never been to

> *I was going to say. What about bacon butties?*

I've got to the point where I'm so bored of sex anyway

> *Pretty damn funny!*

I come from a backwater called Torquay

I don't care what you say

I don't usually speak like this. I've got a funny throat

Good job you didn't hear what he said because it was very rude!

I love you

You want someone to be really rude to you, don't you?

Going back to Torquay is impossible now. Not because of the peace and quiet because I love peace and quiet — but because I can't communicate with the people

Like a fool I said Yes. Then I had to ring back and say No

I started to tell you this a moment ago

There are lots of blokes about like that, aren't there?

[56]

She was a bit drunk, mind you

My mother is totally dependent on me

My ex-husband hasn't given me a birthday present

She tells me she's still nuts about him

*Darling, there were two hazelnuts in the washing machine this morning! You have **got** to check Otto's pockets!*

What does your mum make of the whole thing?

She boozes, I can tell you. Pitches for very expensive drinks

Tough luck!

I know it's boring but, otherwise, the machine is going to break down far sooner than it should!

Dear me!

Loch Ness is mighty deep. There could be two or three monsters down there

Are you pulling my leg?

It's pretty pricey, I should imagine

It's not just the day-to-day living. It's
things like water rates for two hundred
quid. I mean, how are you meant to
pay that?

How can I charge less?

I got into a terrible stink on Tuesday

*I was aghast this morning. I had to
take the car in for a service and my
toes were nearly frozen off as I
waited for a taxi*

The door slammed on me and took the
top of my finger off

*I like shopping. I like spending
money probably*

Don't quote me, for Christ's sake!

*I'm not swimming today. Because
I've hurt my head. I almost killed
myself two days ago. It's so
awful!*

[58]

I thought we'd have chutney,
mayonnaise and salad

> *I'm worried all the time. I'm
> worried every time I pick up the
> phone*

Oh, my God, I can't believe it!

> *I've met her once. What more do I
> have to say?*

If you can afford to pay the gas and
electricity then you're laughing!

> *If my memory serves me right I don't
> think I've ever known it so cold*

Spurs walloped Chelsea seven–one!

> *Sweetheart, could you very kindly look
> up a telephone number on my desk?*

She works her arse off fourteen hours
a day

> *He really is the most boring man I
> know*

I think there was a problem in that
area, as a matter of fact

Poor old you! What a shame!

What's the news on your mortgage?

I was in complete convulsions for half an hour

To tell you the truth, I think he's a little bit on the gay side. To put it mildly

Begin again. Slowly

That's the rumour I've heard. I might be wrong

How long have you known Percy?

I asked 'What's that little dog's name' and she got all terribly offended

She must be hopping mad!

Belief in oneself. That's what it boils down to

There's nothing worse than a smelly dog!

Give me a bleedin' break, won't you?

Practice makes perfect, as they say

I WILL PAY FOR THE TAXI

In a way, that's a compliment, isn't it? A compliment to your hospitality

They play football like a load of wankers!

I still think the smell of soap in clothes is rather nasty

He's the campest thing ever!

This guy at work says it's an all-out bus and tube strike just to fuck everybody up

In the long run it's stupid but there we are

There's this bloke at work — I swear to Christ this is true — who's worn the same suit every day for the last six months!

You better meet this woman I know

I hope you know what you're doing

Now what was I saying before I was so rudely interrupted?

Besides which, I've got a lot of work to do

*He works so damn hard **and** he's got a meeting at five o'clock tomorrow morning*

I must go and get some sleep!

You'd have had heart failure on Friday night

I probably won't sleep a wink tonight!

He's just a bit stressed about things

Just to be safe, get three ketchups!

My sister-in-law is now learning to drive

I'm going to Argentina in February. And Thailand in June. Not bad?

[63]

It's non-stop rain here

Reception's a bit shitty in the cottage

> *You're probably still doing the
> school run. I'll ring you in a
> minute. It's ten past nine*

Whereabouts d'you live?

> *Then she told me the news about
> Dick and Mick getting divorced at
> the same time!*

So you're not far from Gravesend?

> *SORRY, I'LL SHUT UP IN A
> MOMENT*

Say again?

> *I'm just hopping on a bus! I'll
> buzz you back in a moment!*

I'm still getting the same train from
Paddington, which arrives at Torquay
at eleven ten

> **I'm just outside your house!**

I get very scared of
things like that

I was doing cartwheels!

Are you on your own?

Obviously, you know I'm pregnant

I remember you saying!

*That apple crumble thing would be
fantastic!*

I'm not fussy. I'll go with the flow

You know what Shakespeare said!

By the time William's on his fifth
double vodka!

*Can you ring me on my mobile?
I'm in the area*

I'll get there early and try to bag a
window table

*Thank you for your message about
the packed lunch but I would like
to speak to you before you go out*

Okay. I'll catch up with you then

> OKAY. I GET THE PICTURE.
> I'M NOT WANTED

The guy next to me was mopping his
face with a hanky

> *Has anything transpired that makes
> you feel it's going to happen?*

I have a wardrobe of clothes at home I
can't get into

> *Loads of companies go bankrupt*

So sorry. I didn't mean to upset you

> *I'm an only child. There's only me
> and my mother*

I think the price was what put me off
at first

> *You didn't upset me. You
> aggravated me!*

GET LOTS OF CHEESE!

> *Yes, please!*

[67]

He just sits there and eats crap!

> *Did your mum just have the one son?*

I'll give it a go!

> *She used to work in the café next door. She was lovely*

He lives in this really nice studio in Chelsea

> *What's wrong with that?*

I don't know where she's disappeared to

> *As far as I'm concerned no one can ever come near Tommy Cooper*

I do have a few concerns about Gordon. I think he may be a little bit lonely at the moment

> *YOU'RE ALWAYS ON THE BLOODY TELEPHONE!*

If you'd started to laugh, I would have fallen apart!

I've just had a
nasty thought

*I ended up at the emergency dentist
with terrible toothache*

He couldn't have been sweeter, actually

I can't imagine anything lovelier

Are you drunk?

Shouldn't laugh!

I just wondered if you're around
tomorrow morning before we head off
to Haslemere?

*Just ringing up to find out how it
all went*

Most solicitors I know are unbelievably
indiscreet

*Where d'you think I could go and
have a pee?*

Charlotte's now come and told me
she's pregnant

He's been like a brother to me

I'LL GET THE BLOODY FOOD

So?

That car is a disaster area!

> *It's five o'clock. I'm awfully sorry to have delayed ringing you back but here I am now and let's talk soon*

The floor of the front seat was full of water. The boot wouldn't open. The lights weren't working. The brakes weren't working! I mean, brilliant!

> *Okay, darling, see you later, see you tomorrow*

She's now gone and got herself pregnant

> *There isn't any problem mechanically. It just needs some cosmetic attention*

Listen to me, you fool!

> *Every baby's the most beautiful baby. So you're an auntie, then?*

I hope you know what you're doing

If I was going to have a baby, it
would be a total accident

He seems a nice
guy. Underneath it
all, he's horrible

Don't overdo it,
though

He failed his chemistry. It really pissed
him off

He was going up to Fort William,
wasn't he?

You've got a better memory than I
have

The situation could be far, far worse

DARLING, I'M DESPERATE! I'VE
LEFT MY PASSPORT BEHIND!

I'm glad you're looking forward to
moving forward constructively

I'm afraid I'm going to have to cancel
lunch

[72]

Next week's going to be a nightmare!

My view of the Resurrection is much more complicated than it was when I was younger

> *You haven't been in your new house long, have you?*

Most people feel threatened when I tell them my theories about food

> *He's sold his Jag and bought an old Austin Allegro*

I haven't moved in yet!

> *It's so funny. I had you on my list to telephone!*

And the funny thing is she was ringing me at the same time on another line!

> *I've never seen such detailed X-rays before*

I'M DESPERATE! I CAN'T FIND IT ANYWHERE! PLEASE, PLEASE, PLEASE CAN YOU RING?

I live in hopes!

*I think Colin and I will get on
better once we've had a full-blown
bloody argument*

Incidentally, would you like a
dachshund puppy for only twelve quid?

That's the least of my problems!

She's been putting things off until after
the wedding's over

That's stating the obvious!

He used to be a neighbour of mine at
Wembley Park

I'm outside the zoo now!

**Anyway, the wife stormed into the
bedroom**

I think his wife's called Gloria

God, you look far younger than that!
I'm not joking!

*They looked at me as if I was
round the twist*

*I'M NOW OFF TO
THE AIRPORT AT
LAST! SEE YOU IN
APRIL! YES, IT WAS
IN MY BAG ALL
ALONG!*

I made a bit of a cock-up. I was so
bloody tired

> *Now d'you promise me you'll do
> this?*

You ask a lot of questions, don't you?

> *Tomorrow's an absolute horror for
> me. I'm literally out all day*

Sorry, I didn't recognise your name

> *The whole scenario sounds very
> colourful*

What's she ever done for me, I ask you?

> *This weather's getting me down*

Then I twigged who it was! Peaches
Geldof!

Don't ask silly questions!

So you'll be living in Blackpool
permanently, will you?

*The ideal way is to make it profits
oriented*

Barbara's been getting her knickers in a
twist about it

Dear me!

Just to say I've found Blossom's slippers!
They were in the back of the car!

FUCK! FUCK! FUCK! I'VE
JUST SEEN A MAGPIE!

You never know your luck

*Let me know if you need any moral
support*

I'd best go!

Well, if you insist!

I've just remembered that
guy's name. Tom Reed

*Did you hear that Mummy's found
your slippers?*

Isn't that incredible, this day and age?

*I'm trying to find someone called
Tom Reed*

I keep telling you. I'm very disorganised

Well, just as you like!

I try to keep my hanging baskets going
in the winter

*I don't know if you have a number
for him? Or know someone who
does?*

They're now talking about offering
him a directorship

*Before that, I used to think to
myself — you know what I mean?*

She does that regularly, every breakfast
time. Gives me a clout!

*Is that where you get your blue
eyes from?*

[79]

 She was literally curled
up like a snake!

*I thought, Oh, my God,
this is unreal. This is a
nightmare*

So when are you free?

*We're all after the same job, I
suppose*

You're talking nonsense!

It's all rather ridiculous, isn't it?

D'you think you could come this
Friday instead of next?

*That's what her mum keeps saying
to my mum*

Can't you get them to phone you on
Tuesday?

Fuck off!

I could be treading on touchy ground
here, Mary

Do I still have time to have my hair cut?

Funnily enough, me mum used to have a dachshund

This is completely between ourselves

You haven't got the power. You haven't got the acceleration

I'll just see what my four-legged friend is up to

Bloody hell, Jimmy, it's ten past nine!

Blimey! He doesn't hang about, does he?

Did you go and have your hair done yesterday?

Sorry, I'm lost to the world at the moment

If it takes two to five working days, surely it'll be here by Monday?

I was watching it last night – and cracking up!

Bloody hell! What's-his-name? It's gone out of my head now

Hold on a minute! Hold on a minute!

How are you doing? I just wondered

What did you want to say?

How the fuck are you going to do that?

I put the laptop underneath your thing, like you said

Did you hear what I said?

He's going to win the lottery next week, he's assured me that. If he wins ten million we can have a couple of drinks on him

It's outrageous, isn't it?

It's up to you

I'm just going to have a little walk-around

Absolutely bloody useless

I don't know yet

> *I've just had a nasty thought*

Now that I've told you what happened
in Paris, do you still trust me?

> *I'm afraid I can't tell you the
> answer to that question*

What does she say about me? Same old
rubbish?

> *Where are you, my darling?*

I laughed at myself yesterday

> *Midnight to eight is the best shift.
> Nuts calling in, always drunk*

I telephone three hundred people
before I do anything

> *People call up to ask, oh I can't
> remember now, the stupidest
> questions*

She hasn't changed, our Annie

Look, I don't think you're being wholly fair

What's your minimum delivery?

That would be really kind of you. Thanks, mate

Excellent!

What happened? Did she break her wrist?

You have to take the rough with the smooth in life. It's not everything for everybody

You didn't tell me she broke her wrist!

She says she's leaving in a minute to pick us up

Oh gosh!

There's a nice place just across the road

What's the time now? A quarter to eleven!

We were just in shock. We didn't say anything

He's now based out at Staines

I'll have to sign up to all the Chinese networking sites

When the police car arrived it did put a dampener on things

It's going to really stress me out. Just after the weekend in Berlin

I was hoping to be with you by half nine

When I was away I thought I hated London. Now I'm back, I love it!

Hi, Mummy! I'm on the Underground. Where are you?

I'D LIKE TO APOLOGISE

I'm not being funny but how are you going to cope with a baby and a dog?

He now says he hates babies

What exactly are you accusing me of?

That's quite funny

I think you'd be better off offering them a cash deal

Have you downloaded the Dolphin browser?

Think about it anyway

I might just get down there next week

Sounds good!

I only live down the road!

I've just got to Gloucester Road. I'm down at Tesco's right now

You'd better tell Dot to stop e-mailing me. She's made enough calls

We've both got hangovers. We need something to eat!

Sunday? I don't know what I'm doing on Sunday

[87]

Charlotte won't be doing much
relaxing in August. She's having a baby
in September

> *I'm just trying to make it more
> interesting for everyone*

I'll tell you more in a minute. When
it's quieter

> *I'm just catching the train to Blackpool!*

He's in a time warp!

> *Keep an eye on him. Make sure he
> comes up to scratch*

I'm going to do a big shop tomorrow

> *Okay, I will see you in, like, three
> minutes*

I suppose I could put one on my
windowsill

> *When I heard him say that, I
> thought bloody hell!*

She may not be lovely and sexy but
she still sells millions of bloody records

*I can't bear the mess
everywhere*

Simon! Hello! How are
you doing?

Don't worry. Don't worry

D'you think there's anything going on
there?

That's good

Yes, well as long as it isn't anything too
sinister

*I'll have a look tomorrow and see
what we can do*

Sounds good to me! Cool! OK, mate
there we go!

Are you in your chambers?

I'M FUCKING IRRITATED

Can you do me a favour later on?

Apparently the Westbourne originally
fed the Serpentine!

[90]

How's your friend?

I'd love to but I'll have to get a
babysitter

*I'll have my mobile and my
BlackBerry on*

The first time I saw this Sarah character −

*Could you e-mail me all your
thoughts on it?*

They lock you in and you can't get
out of it! I'm serious!

*HOW ARE YOU AND
WHERE ARE YOU?*

That was so lucky! I parked on a single
yellow line. No problem! That was a
real piece of luck

We're now entering a new realm

She was, like, the tallest
woman ever!

*I'm just getting a taxi to
Vogue House now*

Still no luck getting a babysitter but
I'm working on it

I've got my dates mixed up again

My memory's as bad as yours

I feel so much better

I beg your pardon?

Speak to you later. Bye!

I feel my whole life is falling apart

*I've now got a big matted lump on
my head*

My ex and *his* ex have now got
together!

You're a liar!

I've got a cancellation for four thirty
this afternoon. Any good?

Hold on. Say again?

I need to get these done very urgently.
So I'm going to be a bit late

*It's a funny old
set-up there, isn't it?*

Stop ranting at me!

*A small Americano,
she usually has*

OK, Dot, bye!

**It's like the weirdest place I've
ever been in**

Everything all right, Dad?

*At the end of the day they don't
know anything!*

I'm fine. How are you?

I pity anyone who marries him

I was just wondering if you're planning
to bring a lot of luggage

*I've probably missed you. I'll try
you again later*

I'm on my way!

You're being deliberately vague

[94]

I told him I don't give a shit, mate

They're now looking at renting a car

There's something I forgot to say this morning

I can't remember how much we said last time

She's got fantastic contacts, let's face it

I don't know what to do

Oh, gosh, I haven't heard of her for a long time

I was going to call you tomorrow

You needn't say a word

The whole project got shelved

It's a free world. You can do what you like and I have no right to object

Do you understand what I'm trying to say to you?

Don't involve me, darling, for Christ's sake

Has the same thing ever happened to you?

Things have got very expensive lately

I texted her back but she must be away. She does go away quite a lot

It's nice to know you've got a little bit of money

Okay, so one's vaguely available

Sadly I didn't win the lottery last night. I was really hoping to. It would be amazing if I did

It's not much take-home pay, is it?

He's one of the most genuine people I've ever met. I just find him incredibly easy to talk to

I've got just under ten quid to last me to the end of the week

*Did you enjoy being with Tim or did
he make a neurotic wreck of you?*

That's the stupidest question I've ever
heard

*I was in complete convulsions for
half an hour*

He really is the most boring man I know

*When are you and Annie going to
get married?*

I'm not going to divulge any more to you

Great! Well, we'll be in touch later!

Thanks a lot, Dot

*Hello? Tough-going? Finding it
tough? Well —*

Excuse me literally one second

*Fucking hell! I didn't even know
he was still alive!*

She's obviously done very well for herself.
And a lot of it her own hard work

You've still got to pick up the kids at three o'clock

We had ten or twelve days camping. In the middle of Kenya. Every location was different

You told me you'd phone me back and you never did!

I've got to go, man. Got work to do

That's why I'm asking

That's fine

D'you reckon Sheila would be working normal hours now?

That's another possibility

There are too many ifs and buts

My dad does all the peeling and the chopping and the mashing

Fab! We'll be with you in about five minutes!

I'm a bit shell-shocked actually. I hadn't heard back from them for several days then, all of a sudden – I get a text saying it's being delivered today

> *Foxtons the estate agent called me back! They need an office co-ordinator!*

How can people live like that? I just can't understand it

> *Where are you now?*

Sometimes, when you least expect it, it starts snowing

> *Do I turn into Nightingale Avenue?*

I'm not going to be pushed any further. Let bygones be bygones. That's what I say

> **What d'you think I should do?**

Then she cried and wanted more. She does this. She wanted an adult portion. Then she forgot all about it!

Plus, it's embarrassing

No, it's your husband!

I'm not feeling too well at the moment

Did she go to bed okay?

Now granddad seems to have fallen asleep. I'd better not leave him here

You love him, don't you? I can see you do. You do, don't you? Don't you?

Which I must say astonished me

Twenty-five years I've known Beverley

Anyway, I shall keep that under my belt for the moment

It's not that difficult to get one from the council

Some people have got a nerve

Some people always think they know the truth

This is completely mad!

**Mind you, I don't think it's nearly
as cold today as it has been**

Anyway, I won't hold that against you

*Anyway, I won't keep you. Just to
let you know you're in my thoughts*

You mean this week?

Cheeky thing!

Can I help at all?

*Did you end up talking to Ian
Irvine?*

You know that one you bought at
Sainsbury's? The garlic whatsit?

Don't be so angry all the time!

Thursday, it poured with rain

*I've only rung up to
say thanks for a
marvellous meal*

**Don't quote me, for
Christ's sake!**

[103]

You don't listen to a word I say!

Well, just as you like

I gather Mary's spoken to you again

*I met him in the street the other
day. He hadn't time to talk.
Neither had I*

I don't know whether to believe you
about last night. I didn't hit you,
did I?

*God, I haven't thought about that.
Let me have a ponder*

And then we all went to Carluccio's
for sorbets and ice creams

I didn't hit you, did I?

You're obviously not in. I'll try you
again later

*If you phone me on the landline,
it'll be cheaper*

Me again! Sorry!

[105]

*I'm just so sad we aren't fighting
this battle together*

I feel nice because I've just put a nice
clean jumper on

I shouldn't worry yet awhile

Suits me!

I hope I get back before she gets in

Then there's a bit of concrete under
the living-room window which will
look stupid like that, won't it?

Life's too short

But you're not on e-mail, are you?

*D'you remember the place where we
had that meal with Russell?*

I just find it very, very hard getting to
pillar boxes!

She's worth her weight in gold

The timing seems so peculiar

She's a naughty little thing!

[106]

I'M NOT BEING FUNNY

*The thing is not to worry when you
fuck up*

I'm afraid I've got lots of work things
tonight

This evening's going to be a riot!

I've stupidly just realised that I don't
get back from Germany till about nine
that night

*I only went to them because my
other solicitors were so bad*

You surprise me!

*I'm getting a bit cheesed off living
in Wimbledon*

Best of luck! I'll keep my fingers
crossed for you!

You know the man I mean?

I came twice to house. I find no one
in. I wait till ten o'clock. Sorry!

WELL, LEAVE ME
ALONE THEN!

Could I just say two
sentences?

*And you'll be glad to hear we're
having rump of lamb!*

You gave me such a fright!

*Snuffle, snort. Have you got a cold
as well? Is everybody ailing?*

I haven't the remotest idea, I'm afraid

That's exactly what I mean!

Tell me mum I'm all right

*No, seriously, Geoff, think about
this*

Now you know why I gave up
chemistry at school!

*I met someone who knows you. Ian
Irvine*

Why did I think he was called Mark?

He's one of the few people who
makes me laugh out loud

Is Posy coming tonight?

Good luck, I said!

You reckon you're educated?

You were pretty tiddly last night

I thought you said Fuck

I'm sure you're far too busy to talk
so don't bother to ring back

Okay, sweetie

I can't bear lies. I've never lied to
anyone in my life

How's Roger? Is he well?

Other than you

I'm sorry. I meant to
tell you this yesterday

*It's getting up at four
o'clock in the morning
that does me*

It's only my personal
opinion

I think that might be arranged

She's incredibly happily married. Which
surprised me enormously

*She didn't take a damned bit of
notice!*

May I make one tiny little suggestion,
which you're quite at liberty to ignore?

*I know I should have got sliced
bread last night*

And would you believe it? Outside toilets!

*That sort of thing makes one sick
even in ordinary private life*

It's absolutely beautiful outside!

***It's the most boring book I've
ever read!***

[110]

Bear with me one second

I said No – and that's final

Have you done your exercises?

I couldn't give a fuck!

*He'll have to get back to me
immediately. Or there are going to
be mega problems*

I told you. I couldn't give a fuck!

*I'm not going to speculate on her
motives*

Oh, my God, I've just seen my
ex-husband!

*I've got everything like sausage
rolls. Which can sit around on
plates. Frozen*

**Oh, my goodness, he's
literally spewed all down
himself!**

Don't talk rubbish!

In all honesty I could probably do with a little bit of help

They've completely gutted it!

That was exciting, wasn't it?

What's-his-name now blames you

If I sold my house in Wales, I could stick the money in a bank and –

Now do you promise you'll do this?

Pete is calling me less and less

Such a great guy!

And then we watched the most boring film I've ever seen

You make it sound like so much fun

I'm moving houses as well. So it's an absolute nightmare

Is that for medical reasons?

[112]

Don't bother. If it's an awful nuisance,
don't worry

> *I'm afraid that woman is the kiss
> of death on any enterprise*

Hi, sweetie-pie, it's just me, Annie,
checking where you are

> *I just want to get it over and done
> with*

I think that's the worst advice possible

> *There's only so much I can take*

FUCK THIS RAIN!

> *They now think it's a pinched
> nerve*

It all depends on what you want to do
for dinner tonight

> *Which is amazing,
> really, when you look
> at it*

So the paracetamol's
having no effect?

I am exceedingly unenthusiastic
about the whole idea

You're kidding!

What are you going to wear
tonight?

I'm just going to visit my ex-wife

Say no more

I want to stay at home and do nothing
basically

Well, there is that

Let's be honest, you've had six months
to do it

I don't think she knows what's
going on

Hello! Where are you?

No rush, okay?

You haven't let me finish what I was
trying to say

I'll see you when I see you

[114]

A cup of tea would be an absolutely excellent idea

So he's a nasty piece of work?

Yes, they've got a camper van but they've got a tent as well

I've been sleeping with me mate's girlfriend

About time too!

I can't go out any more! I come back dead! I don't know how I did it!

Are you sure?

She gets furious whenever you mention it

At the end of the day, I'm a loser!

And?

I'm off to Italy first thing tomorrow morning

Did I tell you I saw Vanessa Redgrave in Selfridges?

[115]

It's not Annabel I'm worried about. It's Andy. He's a bit of a nutter

ARE WE USING POLYSTYRENE OR PLASTIC CUPS?

I could be persuaded

And?

I'm sure you'll get bored after a couple of minutes

I'll have you know I was sent to a child psychiatrist when I was ten

There you go!

I'll need to learn to speak Thai, obviously

Well, I spoke to Teresa. After she'd spoken to you

How d'you get there, out of interest?

Are you back in her good books?

This is a hopeless telephone call

> *I was thinking about tomorrow.
> I don't know what you've got
> on tomorrow. Have you got any
> meetings or anything tomorrow?*

I think he's on another planet, that man

> *You win!*

Who was that chappie in the shorts?

Jesus Christ!

Maybe it's the cost?

> *Hi, sweetheart, it's me. Just after
> ten thirty. I ended up having a
> very nice cup of coffee with
> Beverley. Which is why I'm not
> home yet but I will be shortly*

Remember, it's Granny's birthday tomorrow!

> *You're a little
> monkey, aren't you?*

D'you know what I'm trying to say?

It's not all about you

The permutations are endless

I'm still three-quarters friendly with him

You've interrupted me in the middle of my lunch

I went down to Church Street and found my car had been towed away!

I feel like a rat in a trap

I like me nights off

This is always a bloody awful time to be in London

I always go berserk when my mother's here!

Sorry?

Bless you, Mary. You've jogged my memory

He was one of the most suburban men
I've ever met!

*Don't **you** start!*

I said if you don't let me in I'll call
the police

*D'you know I'm absolutely frozen
to the gill!*

Don't give me that!

*Her name in Gloucestershire is
absolute mud*

Would you do me an enormous favour?

*Which means we can still submit
the application tomorrow?*

We still need some canapés

YOU'RE WEIRD!

I've got your message but sadly I can't
do tonight. I've got a staff dinner

*There's nothing to worry about at
all*

[119]

I'm still taking a lot of painkillers

I don't know what came over me all of a sudden

You're coping brilliantly!

I'm really sorry but I'm not going to be able to make it tonight

It's very embarrassing but it wasn't my fault

I'm very worried because your mother-in-law hasn't showed up

I imagine you've got your hands full

I think you should pursue this man Richard Brown

You won't believe anyone could be so stupid but I can't find the house I'm meant to be going to!

She always says that

I've got a feeling something's very wrong

Otherwise I'll try you at work
tomorrow

> *Sounds like you've both gone to*
> *bed*

Apparently Nicholas now has a septic
foot

> *You're probably asleep or something*

Is there anything you need me to get
from Waitrose?

> *It's Thursday afternoon and I need*
> *your help*

He is driving me absolutely mad!

> *What?*

Ring me if you want more details

> *I just wondered if you*
> *got my e-mail?*

It's turned out Edward's
got a poetry reading that
night

I just wanted to drop off the washing

Unfortunately we'll have to say no

Anyway –

In about half an hour's time I shall go home

> *It's looking quite likely at the moment*

You were rather irate this morning

> *I'm still trying to finish this high calorific drink*

Unlike him to be out

> *And did I tell you? Outside toilets!*

How are you doing?

> *Oh, my God, now I've spilt it!*

He sounds bad news

> *It's only the arc-welders in the middle of the night that do my nut*

[122]

Don't you lose your temper!

Stephen, I know you're very, very busy but...

Why did you text me on Saturday?

GET LOST!

This always happens at the last minute

I want to talk to you about a friend of mine who hand-paints china

They always say that

Is he still banging on about Tommy Cooper?

Everything is so correct. It's a pain in the neck

Sheila, are you all right regards time?

I had some very good news the other day

You've got a better memory than I have

Yesterday was beautiful

I'll take your word for it

I smoke when I'm nervous. Not at
other times

    *That's a super bit of useless
    information*

Can you give me a buzz and let me
know what you think?

    We'll speak at some point

Any more questions?

    Forgive me

I'll be all right in a second

    Sad news about Andy Williams

He suddenly realised if he went on
grabbing women like that he'd have no
friends

    *When will I get that payment? The
    lump sum?*

At your wedding he was in fine form

*So what happens? The doorbell
rings?*

I'M RUNNING LATE!

So we'll speak at some point?

Weird bastard!

My mum and dad are splitting up

I was fiendishly delayed en route to
Sylvia's. I'm now running an hour late!

They'll be bankrupt before long

So how d'you like being back in
Torquay?

**I was on to the soft drinks by
this time**

We stopped at a bar where we all piled
out to have a pee. An hour later, these
guys were busy negotiating with these
women. They wanted thirty-five
thousand pesetas!

Meaning what, exactly?

> *We decided for all of us that was*
> *quite reasonable. It was hysterical!*

The whole blooming lot wants
renewing

> *I'm an art nouveau fan from way*
> *back*

Bye-bye. You too!

> *I think I'll have an early night*

There are certain subjects which I
don't discuss, as you know well

> *How's Gloria?*

**Why do I keep seeing single
magpies?**

> *He just walked in one day. The*
> *Japanese Ambassador!*

Today's gone potty

> ***I rang him up to give him a***
> ***good bollocking!***

I've figured it out at last

Would you do me an enormous favour?

*The moment I left there was a
police whistle and guess who shot
by? Camilla! Under armed escort!*

One little slip, mate, and you've had it

I'm serious about all this

By the way, we've decided **not** to go
to South Africa. Not this year anyway

Does Ishiguro pop in at all?

This always happens at the last minute

Look, we're literally across the road!

This is absolutely not a criticism but...

*I could have ended up breaking my
ankle **and** my leg!*

And dachshunds have weak backs,
haven't they?

I'm really pissed off!

There's nothing that I can do personally

Is he still with that frightful, ghastly woman?

You're going from one extreme to another!

To be honest, I'd rather not

Pete hasn't got a clue!

This is a mad time to ring me

Can I make a suggestion?

So what are you saying now?

I'm enjoying myself so much. I'm afraid I'm going to turn my mobile off!

Speak for yourself!

I may ring you again tomorrow if you can bear it

A likely story!

He looks a million years old now!

There was no foundation for any romance. She could see I was perfectly happily married

[128]

The fact that you still wake up every morning is wonderful

> *Even if she's abroad, her mobile will still work, won't it?*

May I say one last thing?

> **You know I don't like mashed potato! You know I hate mashed potato!**

I think this conversation had better end right now!

> *But please leave your phone on just in case I need to give you a tinkle*

Hello? All right? Can you hear me?

ABOUT THE AUTHOR

Andrew Barrow is the author of ten books, including *The Tap Dancer*, winner of the Hawthornden Prize, *Animal Magic* and *The Great Book of Small Talk* illustrated by Mark Boxer. His ear for dialogue has been described by Selina Hastings in the *Sunday Telegraph* as 'extraordinary' and by Cressida Connolly in the *Spectator* as 'matchless'.

ABOUT THE ILLUSTRATOR

Posy Simmonds is the author of many books for adults and children, including *Gemma Bovery*, *Lulu and the Flying Babies* and *Fred*, the film of which was nominated for an Oscar. She was made an MBE in 2002 and has won many international awards for her work.

INDEX